# THE CRYPTOCURRENCY INVESTING GUIDE FOR BEGINNERS AND BEYOND

## HOW TO PROFIT FROM THE CRYPTO ASSET BOOM IN 2024 AND FOR YEARS TO COME

By: MATT HOUCHINS

The following work is presented for informational purposes only. None of the information herein constitutes an offer to sell or buy any security or investment vehicle, nor does it constitute an investment recommendation. The information is presented without regard

for individual investment preferences or risk parameters and is general, non-tailored, non-specific information.

While every effort has been made to ensure the

accuracy of the information contained within this report at the time of writing, we cannot guarantee that the content is 100% accurate. We also will not bear any liability in regard to the accuracy of this information, the opinions expressed or any actions you may take based on the contents of this publication.

**Warning: Cryptocurrency investing involves risk of losing some or all of your capital investment. No part of this publication should be considered as financial advice. You should consult your financial advisor before making any decisions on whether to trade in digital currency.**

Hello,

In this book I wanted to give regular people an idea of what Bitcoin and Cryptocurrency are. And some general ideas on how to Profit off of the up and coming Digital Trend from someone just like you. When I started I had no idea what I was doing, but I made money anyway. That's why I am so sure that you can too.

Bitcoin is gaining traction and now you can even buy it through your regular brokerage account.

You might say, I never heard of that, well there are several options to get exposure to bitcoin using just about any brokerage account.

Here are the ticker symbols for 2 of them.

First is GBTC or the Grayscale Bitcoin Trust as of this writing it is trading at around $38, each share of the trust is about 0.001 of a bitcoin, so right now you could buy shares of this trust at a discount of around $9 per share to the current price of Bitcoin which is just over $47,000, that is a 19% discount to the current price.

The second one is Ticker symbol BITO which is a Bitcoin Strategy ETF or Exchange Traded Fund. This fund uses Bitcoin futures to track the ups and downs of the price of Bitcoin. So there you have it, 2 ways to buy Bitcoin in your regular brokerage account, pretty cool, right

As a gift to you for buying and reading my book,

I want to give you a copy of my new report: Top 10 Cryptos to Own For The 2024 Bitcoin Halving, just click here to get your copy of the Free Report.

# Table of Contents

# Introduction

Let me introduce myself, my name is Matt and I have been a crypto investor since Nov. of 2016, when I first bought $500 of ethereum when it was $10. During that bull (up) market of 2017, ethereum soared and went as high as $1,500 before crashing 90% back down to around $150.

After that I was hooked, during that big move in cryptos, I took profits of many times my original investment capital and still held a portfolio of around 15 coins.

My portfolio soared to around $80,000 and then subsequently crashed around 90% to a low of $8,000 in the crypto winter that followed.

So, I know a thing or two about losing in cryptos. I have made and lost a large amount of money riding the ups and downs of the crypto market ever since.

Let me warn you it is not for the faint of heart, it will test you in ways that you can't even imagine now, but it is an amazing ride.

This is why I want to share with you my #1 Rule of crypto investing…..**Never risk more capital than you are willing to lose**.

Do Not invest your rent money or any money for that matter that you need to pay your bills. Only use capital that is extra money or play money, so that if god forbid, you lose it all;

it is only a small portion of your investments. I'm going to advise everyone to not invest more than 5% of your investing capital into cryptos.

So, if you have investments of $50,000 then you should not put more than $2,500 of your investment capital into cryptos.This might not seem like a lot, but you get an incredible bang for your buck investing in cryptos.

Now that you know a little bit more about me…on with the book!

You've most likely seen mentions of bitcoin increasing on news and technology sites in the last few years. bitcoin, along with many others, is a virtual currency, designed to be independent of any individual country or government.

With the ongoing rise in ecommerce and electronic payment  forms, it was perhaps inevitable that currency itself would turn  digital. Even the US Federal Reserve has created a digital payment system called Fed Now, that was implemented in many institutions in late July of 2023.

The value of Bitcoin as well as many alt coins has skyrocketed since it began, which has led to many people getting excited about how they can cash-in on the trend.

This book aims to explain some of the core concepts behind cryptocurrencies, and dispel some of the myths too. We'll also, of course, look at how you can make money in this new market.

# What is Bitcoin

In October 2008 a link to a mysterious White Paper appeared online titled: A Peer- to-Peer Electronic Cash System, it was posted to a cryptography mailing list by the author of the paper named Satoshi Nakamoto.

Nakamoto implemented the bitcoin software as open-source code and released it in January of 2009. Since the code is open source it was transparent and anyone could see it. The identity of Nakamoto is, to this day, still unknown. There are many theories of who Nakamoto is and if he is actually a group of developers, but we may never know the answer.

A Blockchain system would be the backbone of the new digital currency called Bitcoin. A blockchain is a digital ledger of transactions that is replicated and distributed across a network of computer systems to secure information.

The full technical explanation of how Bitcoin works would take a degree to understand, so we'll stick to the basics that you need to know. Bitcoin is a digital currency, which has no affiliation to a country or government. It is a global currency, with the aim of allowing transactions worldwide to be made quickly with minimal fees.

A blockchain is used to record all transactions ever made with bitcoin. It is basically a block of bitcoin transactions joined together in a chain, hence a blockchain. Checking this blockchain allows anyones current balance to be checked like a ledger at a bank. It also ensures that any transactions that are being made are definitely authorized by the individual sending the bitcoins using a private key.

A private key is a string of random numbers and letters that is kept private. It is essentially the key that proves you are the owner of the bitcoin and signs and verifies the transaction, so it goes through.

Cryptography is used to ensure the blockchain cannot be interfered with or become corrupted. In addition, Private Keys (like very long randomly generated passwords) are used on every transaction to act as a digital signature for the person spending the bitcoin. This ensures hackers cannot spend your bitcoin.

The whole system runs on a peer-to-peer network, relying on individuals' personal computers and mining equipment, rather than a central data center. This huge collection of individual computers and equipment all process the data needed to ensure the fast running of transactions.

This processing is called mining. Highly randomized algorithms are used to ensure that any one person can never possibly predict or know whose transactions they might be processing. This further removes the possibility of abuse.

As an incentive for individuals to provide their hardware for performing these services, the mining process also periodically mints new bitcoins, and rewards them to the owners of mining equipment.

Bitcoin has defined the maximum number of coins that will ever be produced at 21 million. This keeps it scarce and desirable to own for the general public and investors. As part of the design of Bitcoin, it periodically halves the amount of new bitcoin produced. This makes bitcoin deflationary because the new supply of bitcoin is halved, or cut in half every 4 years or so. By the way the next halving is scheduled to be around late April of 2024.

Why do I mention the halving? You may not know this, but the halving years also tend to correspond to large price rises in bitcoin after the halving has occurred. So, I am very confident that we will finally see bitcoin soar past the $100,000 mark sometime in 2024.

# Buying and Trading Crypto

In order to buy cryptos, you need to find an exchange that is suitable for you and is in your country. Why, my country you ask? because if anything happens to an exchange outside of your home country, you will have little recourse.

We've listed a few of the most popular options in the resource section at the end of this report. Some of the exchanges that I use are Coinbase, Kraken, Gemini and etoro. These days most exchanges will make you sign up with identification and you will have to prove you are who you say you are.

This is called KYC or Know Your Customer. Just like any bank, the US government is requiring Crypto exchanges to comply with these rules or they can't use US dollars to exchange for the crypto or sell the crypto for dollars.

This is usually referred to in crypto as on-boarding, or how you exchange crypto for dollars. Keep in mind other factors as well like:

- What fees do they charge?

- Do they include 2 factor authenticity?

- Is it located in your country?

Once you have decided on which exchange to use, you simply sign up, link a bank account, send some money from the account to your exchange and you are ready to trade some crypto. This is the exact same process you have to go through to trade any other asset like stocks, bonds, or options. You are just using a different broker that is a crypto exchange.

## Circulating vs Total Supply

Another thing you need to know before you start trading crypto is the difference between the circulating supply and the total supply of a crypto. The circulating supply is just what it sounds like. It is the supply circulating in the market right now. The total supply is the total number of coins or supply that will be issued of that crypto.

The reason why this is very important is based on supply and demand, it also prices the coin. Have you ever wondered why some cryptos trade at $100 and some trade at $0.01? It is all based on supply and demand and the amount of the total supply of the coins. The coins with higher prices tend to have less supply, like bitcoin.

Other coins like Dogecoin, have a very high total supply of coins that are or will be issued.

So look at these factors and keep them in mind when you look to buy any crypto. You can find the supply metrics on coinmarketcap.com.

## Trading

As well as checking the current value of Bitcoin symbol BTC, you may also want to see charts of how it has been performing up to now. There are several sites that provide this. You can just google "Bitcoin chart" to find them. Your exchange will usually have charts as well.

When you check a chart, notice if the price over different time frames is rising or falling. If it is rising, we are in a bull (up) market, if it is falling we are in a bear (down) market. Since bitcoin has risen in 2023 from a low of $15,000 and now sits above $42,000 we are currently in a bull market.

Also, know that when you are looking at trading bitcoin, ether or any crypto, on a pro style platform. (Which, by the way, is the cheapest commission way to trade crypto). For example on Coinbase, if you use the advanced trade feature a trade might cost around $0.70-0.90, if you do it on the regular Coinbase platform it might cost $3 or more.

You will have to trade a pair like a currency. As an example BTC - USD if you buy, you are buying bitcoin with your dollars and if you sell, you are selling bitcoin for dollars.

Most traders of any asset lose more than they win, so it is not advisable to constantly trade in and out of crypto. The swings can be very fast and violent, for example a crypto could lose or gain 5, 10, or even 20% in a single day. Plus crypto trades 24/7 and you have to sleep sometimes.

Just acknowledge that sometimes you will miss a big portion of a move, up or down and realize that holding crypto during the bull market is the best way to go.

Here is how I look at crypto trading. I like to buy crypto when it is down significantly, when there is blood in the streets. Remember when FTX went bankrupt? Cryptos plunged, do you know what I did that day? I was buying some of my favorite cryptos on that plunge.

One of my rules for the bear market is that I don't start buying cryptos until they are down at least 60% from their all time highs. Then I buy slowly in increments of $100 or $200 for each buy. When the price recovers, I wait and see if we get another big plunge to maybe 70% down. I keep doing this very methodically during the crypto winter.

Since I am writing this book in December of 2023 and the crypto winter is over, I think you will see a great bull market incoming in 2024, so you may have to wait to pick up cheap coins again until after this run up in prices.

But I believe we are at the very beginning of the Greatest bull market in cryptos ever, so you may want to buy some crypto now and wait for a pullback to buy more later.

Why do I think that? The reason is very simple, it is because big Wall Street players like Blackrock, JP Morgan Chase, Fidelity and more are all getting into crypto. They will very soon, I think, be pushing cryptocurrencies to the masses as a new asset class that everyone has to own.

If these Mega players start advising their clients to put 2 or 3% of their investment capital into the crypto space, then it will boom like never before. As I am writing this the total market cap for all cryptos is a measly $1.6 trillion. Apple alone is valued at around $3 trillion, so there is a lot of room to run in cryptocurrencies.

I know when you first start out buying cryptos, it can be scary, if you never did it before, but it really is no harder than buying a stock using a trading account. If you do it a few times, you will get used to it and will be a crypto pro in no time.

## When to Sell?

This can be the hardest decision to make when buying any asset, whether it is a stock, bond, or crypto. But the best thing to do is form a strategy when you purchase your crypto. How much do you want to make? Is that reasonable based on its past performance?

The way I make these decisions is that I develop a buying plan and a selling plan with any crypto I buy. I'll give you an example, during the last bear market in crypto, I accumulated 60 Solana. I started buying it when it hit around $25 and every time it would go below $20 I bought a little more, this allowed me to accumulate 60. So when will I sell? Right now my plan to sell solana is to start selling it at $500.

I will sell 10 at $500, another 10 at $600 and another 10 every $100 up until I sell my last 10 at $1,000. Why am I doing it this way? Because I am fairly confident solana will hit $500, but I'm not nearly as confident that it will hit $1,000. I think it might, but you never know. Maybe I am totally wrong and it never gets to $500, that is the risk that I am willing to take to get a big payday. And that is how I trade my cryptocurrencies.

# Wallets & Storage

In order to own cryptos, you need to have a virtual wallet in which to store them. When you wish to receive bitcoin (when you first buy it by exchanging another currency) then your exchange will have a bitcoin wallet in your account with the bitcoin that you bought. You can choose to keep the bitcoin in the exchange wallet or you can transfer the bitcoin to another wallet that you control.

I do some of both, but be aware that any crypto that you leave on an exchange is at higher risk of loss. Why is this? Because you could get hacked and your coins could be transferred to another wallet, without you knowing. The exchange could go bankrupt, think FTX and you may not get your money back. Or the exchange could get hacked (less likely) and they may or may not make you whole.

There are many wallets you can use for crypto, some of the wallets I use are Atomic wallet, Mycelium wallet and Xamen, there are many to choose from. You simply download the wallet to your device and set it up. The wallet will set up a Private Key and a Public Key. The private key is how you validate transactions, so you want to write this down and keep it safe.

If you ever were to say lose your phone, you could use the Private Key or Mnemonic Phrase and your password to set up the wallet again on a new device and all of your crypto will still be there. So be sure to write down the phrase or private key and your password. If you lose these vital items and you can't access the wallet, much like a lost physical wallet your cash will be gone, stuck in the wallet forever.

The Public Key is the address you use to send your purchased crypto to. So you download a wallet and when it is set up, you click on receive, say bitcoin. A Public Key of random letters and numbers will be shown, you simply copy and paste this address on the exchange, then you hit send to, in your bitcoin wallet on the exchange and send.

I always send a small test amount to the wallet first of say like $10 and wait for it to show up in my wallet before I send larger amounts of hundreds or thousands of dollars, just to be sure everything is good, you can't be too careful.

The Public Address is where the crypto is sent. Be very careful however that you don't send the wrong crypto to an address of a different crypto, because all addresses for every crypto are different. So you can't send Bitcoin to an Ethereum address, or you will lose your bitcoin and vice versa.

Wallets can be stored online in the cloud, locally on your own computer or smartphone. Just like a physical wallet, if your digital wallet is lost (and there is no backup) then the currency you had within it is also lost. There are pros and cons for each method.

## Cloud Wallet

Most sites, such as Coinbase and Gemini, offer a combined exchange and wallet service, which can save you time and the effort of sending the coins to your own virtual wallet. Just be aware, you technically don't control the crypto you hold on an exchange.

Cloud-based wallets are marginally more vulnerable to attack by hackers. This is due to them being connected to the internet the whole time, and some being well-known organizations are prime targets for hackers. However, most of them are fully aware of this, and employ strict back-up policies to protect from hacking and system failures.

## Local Wallet

Storing a wallet on your local computer can protect you from hackers. However, if you still use the computer to connect to the internet, you are vulnerable to attack while online. However, you are a much smaller target for hackers to consider.

Some desktop wallets require the bitcoin blockchain to be downloaded in order to function, which is a very large download when you initially install the wallet and it can take a lot of time and computer memory.

## Cold Storage

This term was created to refer to when you isolate your wallet from any internet connection. You may place it onto a portable hard drive, USB stick, or another computer that is not connected to the internet.

This protects your funds from any kind of hacking or viral infection. However, it doesn't protect it from hardware failure, physical theft, loss, accidental damage or natural disasters unless you take further steps. Like placing it in a fire-proof safe, and inside a ziplock bag for example.

It also means that your funds are not readily

available to spend or trade until you return the wallet to your internet-connected computer.

## Emerging Crypto Usage

While Bitcoin has made a lot of sense to many people since it was first launched. It has taken until recently to become mainstream enough to see real-world applications.

Initially, it was accepted by only very tech-savvy websites. Unfortunately, by nature some of these were less reputable than they should have been.

An ever increasing number of online stores are starting to accept Bitcoin and other cryptos. This includes some of the major gift-card retailers, which means you can (in a sense) use bitcoin to pay for items from any number of stores that don't directly take the currency.

Bitcoin ATMs that you can put money in and buy bitcoin or will dispense local cash converted from bitcoin accounts have also been popping up all over. The first was placed in Canada in October in 2013, more and more you will see them in your neighborhood.

Most are using cryptos for investment, not to buy and sell goods. As many people just buy and hold, the prices are more likely to rise. Just based on supply and demand, if the supply is more constrained because nobody is selling the price will rise.

This can also work in reverse, as prices rise to a price where people want to take their profits, there is more supply than buyers and the price can drop quickly.

Cryptos are being utilized in many industries such as online gaming, decentralized finance, supply chain to track goods and reduce counterfeiting, smart contracts, internet of things, metaverse applications, NFTs. Eventually everything will be digitized and on a blockchain.

Especially investments like stocks, bonds and real estate, it opens the door to get investment money for just about any project; as an example, an athlete could sell tokens and pay a dividend based on his future earnings potential. The possibilities are endless. And I am quite sure there are applications that haven't even been thought about yet.

# Crypto, the Press and Government Regulation

It's fair to say that Bitcoin has suffered at times from damaging events regarding security and regulation. Some of the major concerns have been surrounding:

- Successful bitcoin thefts from wallets stored online
- Major crypto exchanges becoming insolvent (FTX)
- Countries regulating and outright bans on crypto (China)

There will always be risks of government heavy

handed regulation, which we have seen recently with the SEC going after many crypto exchanges that operate in the US. Several crypto exchanges such as Bittrex closed down operations because of these government lawsuits against them.

This is very stupid, in my opinion because as we saw in China, they banned crypto but that hasn't changed a thing for cryptos. Sure there were some initial price fluctuations because of the ban, but it hasn't changed the adoption of cryptocurrencies.

It just keeps your country from utilizing them and makes those who do, criminals in their own country, for using an emerging asset class against their governments wishes. Also all of the advancement in crypto and any wealth derived from it in the future will be lost by those countries that try to outlaw crypto.

I think that the government here in the US should adopt a reasonable framework for cryptocurrencies, like they have for other asset classes. This emerging technology is the future of finance.

I do believe that ultimately we will adopt a fair and reasonable framework for this emerging asset class and that when it does come, it will only strengthen the crypto market.

The press has had a love /hate relationship with Bitcoin since it started. They tend to love it when the price is going up and they put on tv, guest after guest, talking about how it is going to the moon.

When the crypto winter takes hold they say it is risky, that Bitcoin is dead and talk about how all these people have lost sooo much money buying the magnificent highs of the last cycle.

However, all of these factors have not caused a total collapse of bitcoin or the crypto market and bitcoin makes a new all time high every cycle. Which tells me there is tons of demand for cryptos in general.

# Crypto Alt-Coins

While Bitcoin certainly takes the limelight when it comes to the press, there are dozens of up-and-coming alternative digital currencies. There are slight differences in how each one works with unique features helping to justify their existence and explain why they might be the next big thing. They are essentially very similar to bitcoin in most respects.

Many traders favor these alternatives (often referred to as *alt-coins*) as they are younger, less saturated and less well-known.

The reason these alt coins are appealing is because a lesser known currency's price is less likely to overreact to breaking news, and can therefore be traded with more predictability.

It also means the price per coin is low, and the scope for supersonic growth (as occurred with bitcoin) is still a possibility. Most of these alternative currency prices will react in relation to the performance of Bitcoin, at least to some degree.

This is because Bitcoin is seen as the flagship cryptocurrency, and faith in that equals faith in the concept in general.

However, some bitcoin price drops are due to specific problems surrounding that currency (that don't apply to others) and this can actually cause a rise in alt prices. In my experience there is a bitcoin market rally first, then as the rally goes too far too fast and starts to correct, we very often will get a rally in the alt-coins.

Where basically investors will sell some of their bitcoin and buy some cheaper alt-coins that they like with their profits. This generally makes the alts move higher and they call this phenomenon an Alt-Coin Season.

# Making Money with Cryptos

## Investment

Given the exponential growth in the value of bitcoin in the years since it was launched, many people have made money simply through buy and hodl investment. (That is not a typo HODL, first appeared in 2013 in an online crypto forum as a typo, for hold, but it soon became embraced by the crypto community. HODL or "Hold on for dear life" is now a widely known concept in the crypto community)

If for example you purchased 1 bitcoin in April 2013, it would have cost you in the region of $100. In December 2023 that 1 bitcoin would be worth $40,000. You could sell it and walk away with around $29,900 in profit (minus any buy/sell fees).

As with any investment, there is always a risk. Some experts say that Bitcoin has survived enough damaging events to be considered safe from a total collapse. But as recent events have shown, hacking, data errors and government policies all have an impact on the trading value of bitcoin.

The right combination of significantly troubling events could still cause the value to crash and possibly never recover, even if unlikely, it is still a possibility.

Others believe that the biggest threat to bitcoin is another cryptocurrency surpassing it as the go-to digital currency of choice.

Regardless of all these what-ifs, the majority of people making money with bitcoin are doing so by simple investments and the buying and selling of the currency.

# Playing the Exchanges

Another tactic that has been mentioned, is what we've called playing the exchanges.

Here you are simply buying and selling a single currency, but you are doing so very quickly and you are selling on one exchange and buying on another.

The idea here is that different exchanges, at any given moment, provide different buy/sell prices for a currency. This is because some exchanges set their own prices, and some take their prices from another authoritative source. Also, different exchanges might update their prices at different intervals, so one might lag behind another.

Let's say you hold bitcoin on one exchange whose values tend to be higher, and whose prices react very fast. You've also found another exchange that is more conservative in their valuations, and are slower to react to big changes in price. For our example, let's say the price has been hovering around $40,000 per Bitcoin for a while on the first exchange. And the more conservative exchange has them at $39,600.

You wait until you see the price rising – and you sell your bitcoin on the first exchange. Let's say they've jumped up to be $40,200 each.

You then move over to the second exchange, and buy the same amount of bitcoin back – before their price has had a chance to start moving with the trend. Their price may still be at $39,600, which means you've gained $400 per bitcoin, but still own the same number of bitcoins.

With a normal currency, this method would rarely be considered, because there is *always* a gap between what an exchange will buy for, and what they will sell for. This is simply how currency exchanges work, and is how they earn their revenue.

However, with bitcoin and other emerging cryptocurrencies, their values can change so fast and so significantly, that there is a much higher chance of you finding a buy/sell price combo that will leave you in profit.

This is added to by the relative youth of the exchanges, and the fact that they don't all operate by the same internal rules.

However, there are still several flaws with this method.

- It's super high-risk. Windows of price difference can close very quickly – especially with such a fluctuating currency value. Plus you are putting into play a large amount, for only a small potential gain.

- Some exchanges also charge transaction fees, on top of the buy/sell divide. This could further reduce or nullify any profit you may have.

- Transactions are not instant. Often transactions can take hours (or even days) to completely go through. Windows of opportunity are not likely to last that long.

- You may need additional capital, because many exchanges use account balances – your initial sale of coins would go into your balance, which you then need to withdraw to your own coin wallet. You would then need to reverse the process to load the account of the second exchange where you wish to make the buy.

It's entirely likely that this would take too long, so you would need to have funds already loaded in the second exchange.

-Your funds end up in the exchange that is more conservative, so if you ever try to move your holdings back to the first exchange (e.g. to try it again) you are likely to reverse some of the gains made originally.

-At the end of it all, you are still only left holding virtual currency, and hence any profit remains virtual too. If the price drops shortly after the buy/sell operation, so will any profit margin you had.

# Playing the Cryptos

As we've mentioned before, there are dozens of cryptocurrencies in existence besides bitcoin. Many experts will hold portfolios of several different currencies at any given time.

By keeping a close eye on each one, they learn to know when a given currency is peaking (has risen, and is likely to fall soon) and when one is in a trough (has fallen, and is likely to rise soon).

Cryptocurrencies (at the present time) tend to behave more like stocks than traditional currencies. Therefore, they are subject to the peaks and trough patterns that stocks often follow. When the price of a stock rises, people are tempted to sell in order to cash in and profit from their holding.

When enough people sell, the price turns and falls. Likewise, when it falls, people see an opportunity to buy at a cheap price. When enough people do this – the price rises. This pattern tends to continue until something major happens that leads to a leap or drop in the price.

Unlike stocks however, cryptocurrencies are not companies, and don't have products or customers. This removes some of the less predictable elements, and makes it somewhat easier to predict their rise and fall.

By swapping their holdings between currencies (buying when low, and selling when high) it is possible to quickly increase the overall value of your portfolio. However, it does require a lot of upfront research, and then constant surveillance of the prices. Plus, of course no single individual can ever predict the future with certainty, and there are still significant risks involved.

# Crypto Dividends

Some currencies you may come across, are in fact more stock like than an actual currency. Some exchanges or forums related to cryptocurrency might launch their own currency, and with it offer dividend payments. The cash raised by this initial sale is treated like an investment in the company and helps to keep them running. The dividends are a way of tempting new buyers.

Similar to stock dividends, these are payouts to all current holders of the currency. For example, one exchange might set aside 30% of all profit to be assigned to dividends and returned to the coin holders. This is done in proportion to the value you own. These dividends are payable to you as long as you hold the currency.

But you are not obliged to retain it, and can sell it at any time. Unless you are investing significant amounts, it's unlikely that dividends alone will provide much of an income boost. However, they are a nice addition to any investment currency that offers them.

# Proof of Stake Coins

There are many alt coins that are called proof of stake coins like Cardano (ADA) and Ethereum (ETH), if you hold it in a wallet on your computer or phone or even on Coinbase, the coin can be staked and you will receive more coins at a certain rate. For ADA the rate is like 5%.

You can then cash out the coins for income or keep adding them to your stash of coins in your wallet after you claim them.I hold several proof of stake coins and I like that you can add to your holdings without actually purchasing more of the coin.

There are numerous proof of stake coins that can be staked in a wallet and you receive more coins as a dividend for waiting for the price to rise in the next bull market. This is a good strategy, if you buy at a cheap price. You get paid for waiting for the price to rise.

# Binary Options

With binary options, you never actually buy or sell the currency itself. What you are doing essentially is placing a bet on how that currency is going to perform. With the rise of Bitcoin, some of the more tech-savvy binary options brokers are adding Bitcoin to their offerings.

A typical binary options trade may look something like this:

-You invest $100 on your trade.
-You choose to trade on the value of Bitcoin
-You choose an expiry time of 5 minutes

-The broker offers a 90% return.

-You then decide whether the value of

-Bitcoin is going to be higher or lower by    the end of those 5 minutes.

For our example, let's say we think it will be higher.

The moment you hit go, the value of bitcoin is recorded, and five minutes later, your trade closes and the new value is checked. If the value of bitcoin is higher, like you predicted, then you get a payout of $190 (your original $100, plus the 90% return promised by the broker).

If the value had actually gone down, your trade would have failed, and your $100 would be lost.

This might seem like a very tempting opportunity, given the high rate of return possible, and odds that appear to be around 1 in 2 of winning. However, if you dig deep into the graph of something like bitcoin to see historically what it has done within any given 5 minute window, you might be surprised.

When you stand back, the bitcoin charts seem to be mostly rising, with a few major drops dotted in. But in reality it is constantly rising and falling – it's just that the rises are ultimately bigger than the falls.

Some brokers offer practice accounts, where you can make dummy trades to see how you would have performed. These are invaluable to give you a sense of how things might go.

Experts say that Binary Options trading without informed advice is just like playing heads or tails. Different brokers have different criteria in terms of minimum account balances and minimum trade values. All brokers tend to offer some kind of incentive or exclusive options in order to encourage you to sign up with them.

Some might offer insurance on your first trade (i.e. you get your money back even if you lose) or they might offer bonus credit for your balance, etc. Sign up and get a 50% Bonus on your deposit At

Pocket Option

# Artificial Intelligence Crypto Bots

Since artificial intelligence has gained traction there are now some exchanges that offer ai bots to trade cryptos. They use a grid based bot that buys and sells the crypto for small profits as the price rises and falls by a preset percent. This is a good option for people who have trouble controlling their emotions and get caught constantly selling at the lows and buying the highs.

The bot takes emotion out of it and will buy on the way down and sell on the way up. And the account will make profits on the trading as well as the appreciation of the coin price. This can be a good way to be able to hold on to a position for a longer term, without getting shaken out by the market ups and downs.

Just be aware that you will not make as much as a simple buy and hold strategy because the bot holds both coins and cash and as the price rises the coins will be slowly sold off and raise the cash position in the bot.

The opposite happens on price declines, more coins are bought as the price slides and the cash position in the bot is lowered. Lately I have been investing a few hundred dollars in a grid bot using the crypto MATIC, it has been showing small grid profits and my account is gaining on an annual basis around 30%.

This is a slow and steady process, but it seems to work well. You can check out the app I'm using here…Sign up for Pionex and try a crypto bot.

# Crypto Mining

As we mentioned before, bitcoin (and many other cryptocurrencies) can be mined by using your own hardware to assist the peer-to-peer processing of bitcoin transactions. These cryptos are called Proof of work coins.

While it is technically possible to use a reasonably powered computer to mine for coins, it is not recommended.

Mining involves running through extremely complex operations, the nature of which requires graphical processors in order to complete them in anything approaching a reasonable timeframe.

Even with a decent gaming PC with above average  specifications, your rate of mining (i.e. the number of coins you can expect to earn in a given time) will be far outweighed by the cost of you doing so (primarily in electricity costs, and secondarily by depreciation in your hardware).

Even if the value of the coins has recently jumped up to a new high – this won't improve matters, because the complexity of the operations tends to increase in-line with the value of the currency. The only way you can earn big from home mining, is to be out of pocket for the electricity costs now, in the hope that you get lucky and score a few bitcoin, which is unlikely.

## Dedicated Mining Hardware

For these reasons, mining is only really performed successfully by dedicated hardware that has been specifically designed for the task. These machines are optimized to perform mining as quickly and efficiently as possible – *and nothing else*. They are not regular computers that you can use as normal.

Serious mining professionals might run a farm of such devices, and the complexity of the setup is out of reach of most people.

## Hiring Mining Hardware

Some companies allow you to hire mining hardware. The machines remain in their server center, but their output is dedicated to you. Again, the fees for this can be costly, and there is often a minimum-term contract involved.

The pros and cons of renting vs. buying are very

similar to those of renting a regular appliance such as a TV.

It will be cheaper to start with, and despite your total commitment (given the minimum contract length) it can still give you some form of a get-out clause before you've spent the same amount as you would have for owning hardware.

The flipside is that eventually, this model turns around. If you continue with renting indefinitely, you eventually will have paid *more* than if you had originally bought your own equipment. Although you will at least be guarded against hardware failure, and may even see your equipment upgraded over time.

I recommend that you perform rigorous research before making a decision to take up mining seriously and don't recommend it.

With the raft of new cryptocurrencies emerging, there may be some that are young enough to mine with a regular PC. But you are banking on that currency later rising in value significantly in order to offset your costs.

# How to Evaluate a Crypto

Everyone wants to know how to evaluate a Cryptocurrency? How do you know if it is a good one to own or if it is a scam? Well the truth is you can never be absolutely sure, but you can use a few common sense techniques that will help you be successful most of the time.

I have invested in many different cryptos since I started in 2016. I currently have around 15 different coins in wallets and on exchanges. I have probably bought over 50 different coins since I started in crypto.

When I was starting out I had no idea what to look for, so I just read the whitepaper and looked online. I quickly realized that many of the online reviewers were hyping coins to either get free coins or to make the coins

they owned increase in value, so they could sell out for a profit.

## Don't Do Any ICO's

What is an ICO? It is an initial coin offering, they also have IEO's now Initial Exchange Offerings. This is the same idea as a stock going public. If it is hyped up enough it will run up, but unless you know it is a good coin with good long term prospects. It will be hard to determine good ones from total scams.

I bought into many different ICO's and usually they initially go up, but then very often come right back down below the original ICO price. They can take a long time for anything to happen and many can't

even get listed on an exchange, so you can't sell

even if you want to. I have waited till months after ICO's to buy when the price crashes to below the ICO price, so be careful out there.

I recommend that you **Do Not** participate in ICO's or IEO's, unless you are pretty sure they will be listed on a big exchange like Coinbase.

Quite a few of them are scams and the US government is making it harder for regular people to get into these now too.

The good news is that even without icos there is no shortage of cryptos to find and buy. There are more than 22,000 cryptos out there now and it keeps on growing.

## Read the Whitepaper and see if it makes sense to you!

This may seem like a no-brainer, but I am sure that tons of people  are just buying coins without reading the whitepaper. Sure you can get lucky and make money in a bull market, but when prices collapse the crap coins will go down the most.

The whitepaper contains all of the info about the project, what they are trying to accomplish, the market they are going into and all of the vital information of the business they are trying to establish. So read it and see if you think they can actually make a business out of their idea.....does the idea make sense to you?

You can download the whitepaper on the crypto's website, you can find links to the sites on Coinmarketcap.com

## Does it make sense as a business? Is there a working product?

Put on your business hat and think about the idea for a second. Does it make sense as a business?

Can they make money selling their product or

service? Do they even have a working product or a service to sell?

If there is no working product, there is no way of making any money until they have a product up and running, **except of course your money.** So you need to be wary of a project that has nothing but a whitepaper, it could turn out to be good. But it won't be for a long time most likely.

## What about the team?
## Do any of them have business experience?
## Or blockchain experience?

The team could make all of the difference, especially if there is no working product. Check them out, do they have links to their Linkedin profiles? If not that could be a red flag. Check out their previous blockchain and business experience. Have they been involved with a successful project before?

If you believe the team can execute their vision and they are really good, then this could be a winning project. If all goes as planned, but expect to wait awhile for it if there is no product. Always check out the team before making a decision to buy.

## Will customers or businesses be willing to pay for the product or service?

If we want to make money we must consider if the product that the project is going to make, will be something people or businesses will pay for. How will they be able to make money on this idea, product or service?

The utility (use) of a coin is very important, if nobody is willing to pay, then nobody will use these tokens and it will eventually die out. We want to buy projects that will have a lot of coin demand, the higher the demand for the coin the higher the price will climb.

Most of the large market cap coins have a good use case. For example, Bitcoin is digital gold, a store of value because of limited supply and you can buy and sell with it.

Ethereum is an improvement on the Bitcoin blockchain, it is much faster and smart contracts can be implemented on its blockchain. ICO's can be launched using ether and its blockchain.

Speculation is not enough, the coin must have a good use case to be successful.

## What is the price? Can you buy it cheaply?

If the price is 50 – 80% off the highs, it may be a great time to buy this coin. But if it is at an all time high or near it you may want to wait for a better price.

The crypto market is very volatile and prices often fluctuate wildly from month to month, so waiting a few weeks and just keeping an eye on a coin you are interested in may pay off huge if the coin drops and you pick it up near the lows.

Very often coins will be listed on an exchange for the first time when this happens there can be a lot of selling as people who bought into the ico cash out.

This often causes the price to be very high at first and drop way down, many times to pennies. I have seen many times where coins drop very near or even below the ico price. That could be a great time to pick up the coins and wait for a rebound in the price.

This is the criteria I try to use to evaluate what coins I buy.

When I deviate from them, I am more likely to lose money in my account. I hope you learned a lot from this and now you are more confident that you will be able to tell a good crypto from a bad one.

# Conclusion

I hope that this book has increased your knowledge of cryptocurrencies and the potential they hold.

While Bitcoin has hit the headlines numerous times in recent years, it is still an emerging technology. As such there remains great potential for those willing to put in the research and take the risk.

As with any high-risk investment, only commit

funds that you can afford to lose.

Remember that with most tactics mentioned here, the worst case scenario is not zero profit, but is the total loss of your original investment.

So be careful out there.

To Your Crypto Success,

Matt

# Resources

## Learning

Official site of Bitcoin

List of All Cryptos, Prices & Market Cap

## Exchanges

eToro

Pionex (Ai Trade Bots)

Coinbase

Gemini

## Binary Options Broker

Pocket Option

## Wallets

Ledger Hardware Wallet (Safest, offline)

Atomic Wallet (mobile wallet)

## Mycelium Wallet for Bitcoin and Ether (mobile wallet)

www.ingramcontent.com/pod-product-compliance
Lightning Source LLC
Chambersburg PA
CBHW070817290526
45795CB00002B/736